Paul de Keyser

Violin Playtime Studies

Really easy studies for the young violinist

with illustrations by Penny Dann

Faber Music Limited

London

© 1988 by Faber Music Ltd
First published in 1988 by Faber Music Ltd
Bloomsbury House 74–77 Great Russell Street London WC1B 3DA
Music set by Musicpage Ltd
Printed in England by Caligraving Ltd
Illustrations © Penny Dann
Cover design by M & S Tucker

ISBN10: 0-571-51013-2
EAN13: 978-0-571-51013-9

To buy Faber Music publications or to find out about the full range of titles available
please contact your local music retailer or Faber Music sales enquiries:

Faber Music Limited, Burnt Mill, Elizabeth Way, Harlow, CM20 2HX England
Tel: +44 (0)1279 82 89 82   Fax: +44 (0)1279 82 89 83
sales@fabermusic.com   fabermusic.com

VIOLIN PLAYTIME STUDIES

In the vast literature for the violin, studies lie midway between exercises and repertoire pieces, encouraging the development of a sound technique. A good study focuses on one particular point, while at the same time maintaining melodic and musical interest.

Violin Playtime Studies is a first anthology of established and newly composed studies for the young violinist. Taking as its starting point the one-octave scale of D major, and remaining in first position throughout, it may be used in conjunction with the *Violin Playtime* series. This combination of short, purposeful studies enlivened by delightful illustrations will ensure that 'study time' is never dull!

Paul de Keyser

CONTENTS

Part I

Part II

Violin Playtime Studies Part I

1. Climbing the D major scale

2. The See-saw

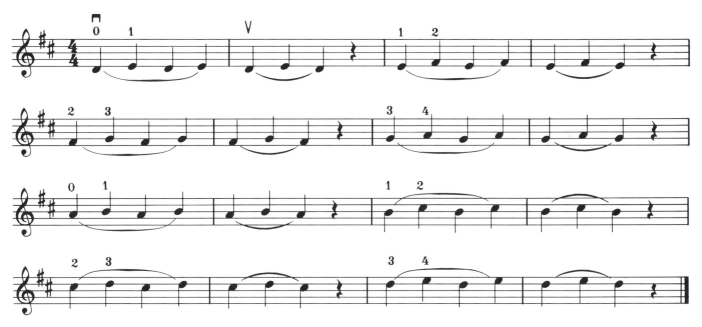

Gliding: Two Legato Studies

3.

4.

5. Birdsong

6. Third Finger Geography

Charles Dancla
(1817-1907)

4

7. Tick-tock Quavers

8. Puppet on 2 Strings

9. G string Ländler

10. Courageous Crotchets

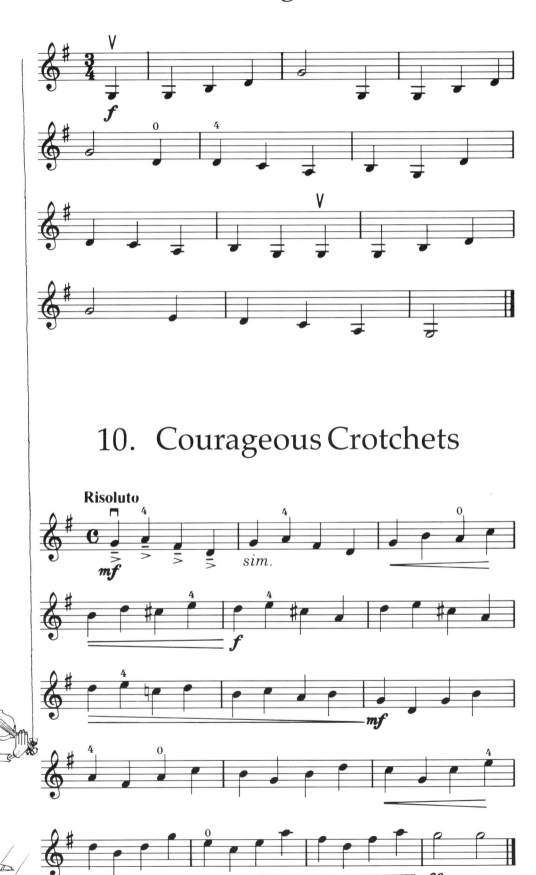

11. Galloping Arpeggios

12. The Bouncing Ball

13. The Little Jester

Johannes Brahms
(1833-1897)

14. Legato Leaps

Dancla

15. Czech Folk-Song

Traditional

Part II
16. Gavotte

G.F. Handel
(1685-1759)

17. Snakes and Ladders

Dancla

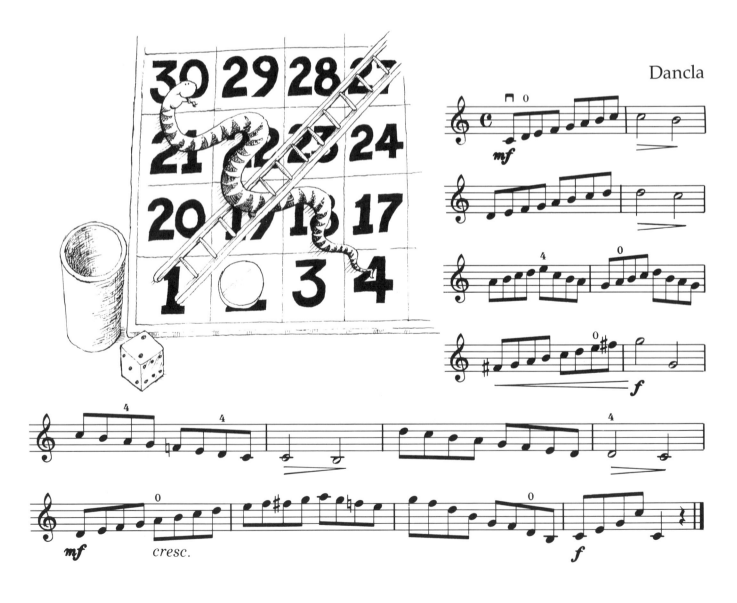

18. Trumpet Tune

19. The Bees' Polka

20. Hornpipe

21. Dreaming

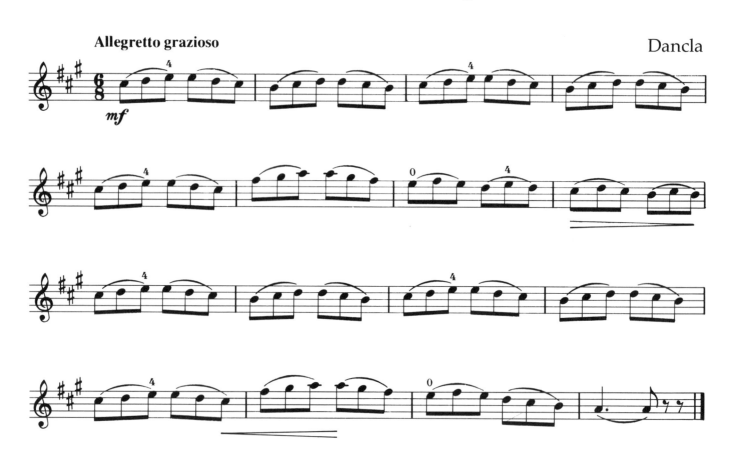

22. On Parade

23. Steeplechase

Dancla

24. Tyrolean Dance

Bartolomeo Campagnoli
(1751-1827)

25. Chugging Along

26. German Folk-Song

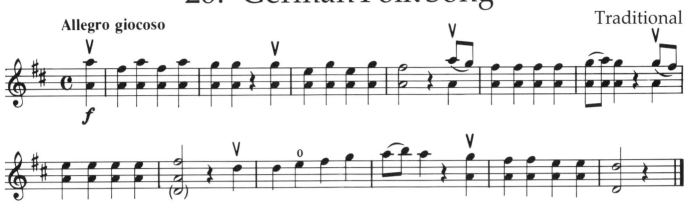

27. Rowing on the Lake

28. The Donkey

29. March

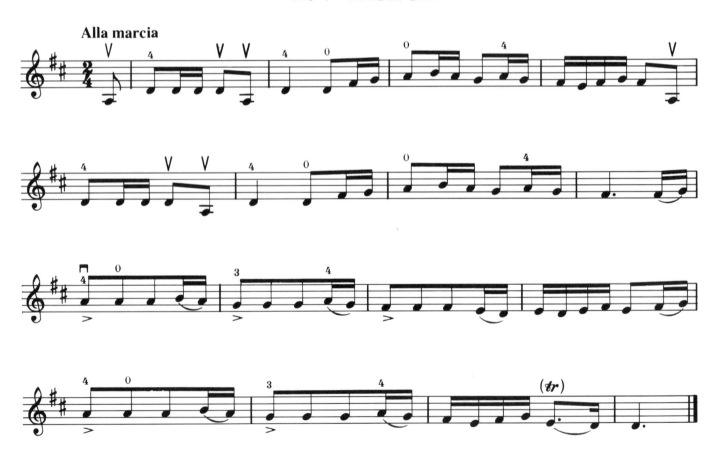

30. Allegro brillante

Louis Spohr
(1784-1859)

VIOLIN MUSIC FOR THE BEGINNER
FROM FABER MUSIC

Jackaroo

Fantastical pieces for the absolute beginner

CAROLINE LUMSDEN and PAM WEDGWOOD

VIOLIN ISBN 0-571-52149-5
Also available:
VIOLA ISBN 0-571-52169-X
CELLO ISBN 0-571-52189-4

Jurassic Blue

Monstrous pieces for the beginner

CAROLINE LUMSDEN and PAM WEDGWOOD

VIOLIN ISBN 0-571-52159-2
Also available:
VIOLA ISBN 0-571-52179-7
CELLO ISBN 0-571-52199-1

Superstart Level 1

Basic skills and pieces for beginners

MARY COHEN

PUPIL'S BOOK ISBN 0-57151319-0
PIANO ACCOMPANIMENT ISBN 0-571-51711-0

Red Parrot, Green Parrot

*A fresh approach to the
young fiddler's first year*

EDWARD HUWS JONES

PUPIL'S BOOK ISBN 0-571-51171-6
TEACHER'S BOOK ISBN 0-571-51008-6

The Young Violinist's Repertoire

*A library of simple classics
for the learner violinist*

PAUL DE KEYSER and FANNY WATERMAN

BOOK 1 ISBN 0-571-50618-6   **BOOK 2** ISBN 0-571-50657-7
BOOK 3 ISBN 0-571-50818-9   **BOOK 4** ISBN 0-571-50819-7

Violin Playtime

Very first pieces with piano accompaniment

PAUL DE KEYSER

BOOK 1 ISBN 0-571-50871-5
BOOK 2 ISBN 0-571-50872-3
BOOK 3 ISBN 0-571-50873-1

FABER *ff* MUSIC